MEDITERRANEAN DIET SNAKS AND APPETIZERS

LEARN HOW TO COOK MEDITERRANEAN THROUGH THIS DETAILED COOKBOOK, COMPLETE OF SEVERAL TASTY IDEAS FOR GOOD AND HEALTY SNAKS. SUITABLE FOT BOYTH ADULTS AND KIDS, IT WILL HELP YOU LOSE WEIGHT AND FEEL BETTER, WITHOUT GIVING UP YOUR FAVOURITE FOOD

Table of Contents

Veggie Chips

Prep time: 10 minutes I **Cooking time:** 30 minutes I **Servings:** 4

Ingredients:
- 1 pound carrots, peeled and thinly sliced
- Salt and black pepper to the taste
- ½ teaspoon rosemary, dried
- 1 tablespoon chives, chopped
- Cooking spray

Directions:
1. Spray a baking sheet with cooking spray, spread the carrots chips, add the rest of the ingredients, toss and bake at 390 degrees F for 30 minutes.
2. Divide the chips into bowls and serve.

Nutrition facts per serving: calories 48, fat 0.2, fiber 2.9, carbs 11.3, protein 1

Rosemary Potato Wedges

Prep time: 10 minutes I **Cooking time:** 35 minutes I **Servings:** 4

Ingredients:
- 2 sweet potatoes, peeled and cut into wedges
- Salt and black pepper to the taste
- 2 tablespoons olive oil
- 1 tablespoon rosemary, chopped
- 2 tablespoons balsamic vinegar

Directions:
1. Spread the potato wedges on a baking sheet lined with parchment paper, add the rest of the ingredients, toss and bake at 400 degrees F for 35 minutes.
2. Divide into bowls and serve as a snack.

Nutrition facts per serving: calories 153, fat 7.3, fiber 3.4, carbs 21.5, protein 1.2

Spinach Dip

Prep time: 10 minutes I **Cooking time:** 20 minutes I **Servings:** 5

Ingredients:
- 4 cups spinach, chopped
- 2 tablespoons olive oil
- Salt and black pepper to the taste
- 4 garlic cloves, minced
- ¾ cup tahini
- ½ cup coconut cream
- 1 tablespoon lime juice
- 1 tablespoon coriander, chopped

Directions:
1. Heat up a pan with the oil over medium heat, add the garlic and sauté for 2 minutes.
2. Add the spinach and the other ingredients, stir, cook for 18 minutes more, blend using an immersion blender, divide into bowls and serve.

Nutrition facts per serving: calories 408, fat 38.5, fiber 5.6, carbs 13.3, protein 9.4

Avocado and Onion Spread

Prep time: 10 minutes I **Cooking time:** 0 minutes I **Servings:** 6

Ingredients:
- 2 avocados, peeled and pitted
- 1 red onion, chopped
- 2 spring onions, chopped
- 1 tablespoon lemon juice
- 1 tablespoon cilantro, chopped
- A pinch of salt and black pepper

Directions:
1. Mash the avocados in a bowl, add the onion, the spring onions and the other ingredients, whisk and serve as a party dip.

Nutrition facts per serving: calories 219, fat 19.7, fiber 7.6, carbs 11.9, protein 2.4

Curry Shrimp Appetizer

Prep time: 5 minutes I **Cooking time:** 10 minutes I **Servings:** 4

Ingredients:
- 1 pound shrimp, peeled and deveined
- 2 tablespoons olive oil
- 2 spring onions, chopped
- A pinch of salt and black pepper
- ½ teaspoon cumin, ground
- ½ teaspoon rosemary, dried
- 1 teaspoon curry powder
- 2 tablespoons chives, chopped

Directions:
1. Heat up a pan with the oil over medium heat, add the spring onions and sauté for 2 minutes.
2. Add the shrimp and the other ingredients, toss, cook for 8 minutes, arrange on a platter and serve.

Nutrition facts per serving: calories 201, fat 9.1, fiber 0.5, carbs 2.9, protein 26.1

Pineapple and Tomato Salsa

Prep time: 10 minutes I **Cooking time:** 0 minutes I **Servings:** 4

Ingredients:
- 2 cups pineapple, peeled and cubed
- 4 scallions, chopped
- ¼ cup cilantro, chopped
- 1 green chili pepper, chopped
- 2 tomatoes, cubed
- 2 tablespoons olive oil
- Salt and black pepper to the taste
- 1 tablespoon lemon juice
- A pinch cayenne pepper

Directions:
1. In a bowl, combine the pineapple with the scallions and the other ingredients, toss well and serve as a party salsa.

Nutrition facts per serving: calories 100, fat 3.8, fiber 4, carbs 8, protein 9

Italian Kale Dip

Prep time: 10 minutes I **Cooking time:** 30 minutes I **Servings:** 6

Ingredients:
- 2 cups kale, chopped
- 1 yellow onion, chopped
- Salt and black pepper to the taste
- 2 tablespoons avocado oil
- Juice of 1 lemon
- 1 teaspoon Italian seasoning
- ¼ teaspoon chili powder
- 1 teaspoon cumin, ground
- 1 cup coconut cream

Directions:
1. Heat up a pan with the oil over medium heat, add the onion and sauté for 5 minutes.
2. Add the kale, the cream and the other ingredients, whisk, cook over medium heat for 25 minutes more, blend using an immersion blender, divide into bowls and serve as a party dip.

Nutrition facts per serving: calories 126, fat 7, fiber 2, carbs 9, protein 7

Coconut Dip

Prep time: 10 minutes I **Cooking time:** 20 minutes I **Servings:** 8

Ingredients:

- 1 garlic head, peeled and cloves separated
- 1 cup coconut cream
- 1 cup spinach, torn
- 1 tablespoon olive oil
- 1 teaspoon rosemary, dried
- 1 tablespoon chives, chopped
- A pinch of salt and black pepper

Directions:

1. Heat up a pan with the oil over medium heat, add the garlic and sauté for 10 minutes.
2. Add the spinach, cream and the other ingredients, whisk, cook over medium heat for 10 minutes more, blend using an immersion blender, divide into bowls and serve.

Nutrition facts per serving: calories 100, fat 3, fiber 4, carbs 8, protein 5

Tahini Peppers Spread

Prep time: 10 minutes I **Cooking time:** 0 minutes I **Servings:** 6

Ingredients:
- 1 cup roasted red peppers, minced
- 1 tablespoon avocado oil
- 4 garlic cloves, chopped
- ½ cup tahini paste
- 2 tablespoons lemon juice
- 1 tablespoon cilantro, chopped
- A pinch of salt and black pepper

Directions:
1. In a blender, mix the peppers with the oil, the garlic and the other ingredients, pulse well, divide into bowls and serve as a party spread.

Nutrition facts per serving: calories 140, fat 6, fiber 2, carbs 9, protein 8

Turmeric Mushroom Spread

Prep time: 10 minutes I **Cooking time:** 25 minutes I **Servings:** 8

Ingredients:
- 1 tablespoon olive oil
- 1 yellow onion, chopped
- 1 pound white mushrooms, sliced
- 1 teaspoon turmeric powder
- 1 teaspoon coriander, ground
- 3 garlic cloves, minced
- 2 cups coconut cream
- A pinch of salt and black pepper
- 1 tablespoon dill, chopped

Directions:
1. Heat up a pan with the oil over medium heat, add the onion and the garlic and sauté for 5 minutes.
2. Add the mushrooms and sauté for 5 minutes more.
3. Add the rest of the ingredients, stir, cook over medium heat for 15 minutes, blend using an immersion blender, divide into bowls and serve.

Nutrition facts per serving: calories 120, fat 8, fiber 5, carbs 10, protein 9

Lime Dip

Prep time: 10 minutes I **Cooking time:** 0 minutes I **Servings:** 6

Ingredients:
- 1 cup coconut cream
- 2 tablespoons cilantro, chopped
- ½ cup baby spinach
- A pinch of salt and black pepper
- Juice of 1 lime
- ½ teaspoon cumin, ground
- 3 garlic cloves, chopped

Directions:
1. In your blender, combine the cream with the cilantro and the other ingredients, pulse, divide into bowls and serve as a party dip.

Nutrition facts per serving: calories 120, fat 12, fiber 2, carbs 11, protein 5

Lime Olives Dip

Prep time: 10 minutes I **Cooking time:** 0 minutes I **Servings:** 8

Ingredients:
- 2 cups black olives, pitted and sliced
- A pinch of salt and black pepper
- 4 tablespoons olive oil
- 4 garlic cloves, chopped
- Juice of 1 lime
- 1 tablespoon cilantro, chopped

Directions:
1. In a blender, combine the olives with salt, pepper and the other ingredients, pulse well, divide into small bowls and serve as a party dip.

Nutrition facts per serving: calories 165, fat 11, fiber 4, carbs 8, protein 5

Coconut Bok Choy Dip

Prep time: 10 minutes I **Cooking time:** 25 minutes I **Servings:** 6

Ingredients:
- 2 garlic cloves, minced
- 1 pound bok choy, torn
- 1 yellow onion, chopped
- 1 cup coconut cream
- 1 tablespoon olive oil
- 1 tablespoon cilantro, chopped
- A pinch of salt and black pepper

Directions:
1. Heat up a pan with the oil over medium heat, add the onion and the garlic and sauté for 5 minutes.
2. Add the rest of the ingredients, stir, cook over medium heat for 20 minutes, blend using an immersion blender, divide into bowls and serve.

Nutrition facts per serving: calories 150, fat 2, fiber 3, carbs 8, protein 5

Walnuts Snack

Prep time: 10 minutes I **Cooking time:** 14 minutes I **Servings:** 4

Ingredients:
- 1 cup walnuts
- 1 tablespoon olive oil
- 1 teaspoon garlic powder
- 1 teaspoon smoked paprika
- A pinch of salt and black pepper

Directions:
1. Spread the walnuts on a baking sheet lined with parchment paper, add the oil and the other ingredients, toss and bake at 400 degrees F for 14 minutes.
2. Divide the mix into bowls and serve.

Nutrition facts per serving: calories 100, fat 2, fiber 4, carbs 11, protein 6

Lentils and Tomato Salsa

Prep time: 10 minutes I **Cooking time:** 20 minutes I **Servings:** 8

Ingredients:
- 1 yellow onion, sliced
- 2 spring onions, chopped
- 1 cup cherry tomatoes, halved
- 1 cucumber, cubed
- 1 cup red lentils, cooked
- 1 tablespoon lemon juice
- ¼ cup parsley, chopped
- 1 tablespoon curry powder
- 1 tablespoon olive oil

Directions:
1. Heat up a pan with the oil over medium heat, add the onion and spring onions and sauté for 5 minutes.
2. Add the lentils and the other ingredients, toss, cook over medium heat for 15 minutes, divide into small bowls and serve cold.

Nutrition facts per serving: calories 142, fat 4, fiber 3, carbs 8, protein 8

Garlic Tomato Salsa

Prep time: 10 minutes I **Cooking time:** 0 minutes I **Servings:** 6

Ingredients:
- 1 pound cherry tomatoes, halved
- 1 cup zucchini, cut with a spiralizer
- 2 tablespoons olive oil
- 3 spring onions, chopped
- 3 garlic cloves, minced
- 2 teaspoons balsamic vinegar
- 1 tablespoon basil, chopped
- A pinch of salt and black pepper

Directions:
1. In a bowl, combine the tomatoes with the zucchinis and the other ingredients, toss well and serve.

Nutrition facts per serving: calories 121, fat 3, fiber 1, carbs 8, protein 6

Masala Dip

Ingredients:
- ½ cup walnuts, chopped
- 1 cup coconut cream
- ½ teaspoon chili powder
- A pinch of salt and black pepper
- ½ teaspoon garlic powder
- 1 teaspoon cumin, ground
- 1 teaspoon garam masala

Directions:
1. In a blender, combine the walnuts with the cream, the chili powder and the other ingredients, pulse well, divide into bowls and serve as a party dip.

Nutrition facts per serving: calories 152, fat 5, fiber 7, carbs 9, protein 8

Sage Dip

Prep time: 10 minutes I **Cooking time:** 0 minutes I **Servings:** 8

Ingredients:
- 1 cup spring onions, chopped
- 1 cup coconut cream
- 1 tablespoon tahini paste
- 1 tablespoon olive oil
- 1 teaspoon sage, ground
- A pinch of salt and black pepper

Directions:
1. In a blender, combine the spring onions with the cream, the tahini paste and the other ingredients, pulse well, divide into bowls and serve cold.

Nutrition facts per serving: calories 112, fat 5, fiber 2, carbs 8, protein 7

Broccoli Dip

Prep time: 10 minutes I **Cooking time:** 20 minutes I **Servings:** 4

Ingredients:
- 1 pound broccoli florets
- 1 cup spinach leaves, torn
- 1 cup coconut cream
- 1 tablespoon olive oil
- 1 yellow onion, chopped
- A pinch of salt and black pepper
- 1 teaspoon smoked paprika
- ½ teaspoon chili powder
- ¼ teaspoon mustard powder

Directions:
1. Heat up a pan with the oil over medium heat, add the onion and sauté for 5 minutes.
2. Add the broccoli, the spinach and the other ingredients, stir, bring to a simmer and cook over medium heat for 15 minutes more.
3. Blend using an immersion blender, divide into bowls and serve.

Nutrition facts per serving: calories 223, fat 18.4, fiber 5.4, carbs 14.3, protein 5.2

Coconut Chard Dip

Prep time: 5 minutes I **Cooking time:** 20 minutes I **Servings:** 4

Ingredients:
- 2 cups chard leaves
- 1 cup coconut cream
- ¼ cup tahini paste
- 1 tablespoon olive oil
- 1 yellow onion, chopped
- 1 teaspoon chili powder
- 1 teaspoon sweet paprika
- A pinch of salt and black pepper
- Juice of 1 lime
- 1 tablespoon cilantro, chopped

Directions:
1. Heat up a pan with the oil over medium heat, add the onion, chili powder and the paprika, stir and cook for 5 minutes.
2. Add the chard and the other ingredients except the cream and the tahini paste, stir, cook over medium heat for 15 minutes more and transfer to a blender.
3. Add the remaining ingredients, pulse well, divide into bowls and serve as a party dip.

Nutrition facts per serving: calories 278, fat 26.1, fiber 4.1, carbs 11.4, protein 4.8

Paprika Seeds Snack

Prep time: 10 minutes I **Cooking time:** 15 minutes I **Servings:** 4

Ingredients:
- ½ cup sunflower seeds
- ½ cup chia seeds
- ½ cup pine nuts
- ½ cup pumpkin seeds
- 1 tablespoon coconut oil, melted
- 1 teaspoon sweet paprika

Directions:
1. Spread the seeds on a baking sheet lined with parchment paper, add the oil and the paprika, toss and cook for 15 minutes at 400 degrees F.
2. Divide into bowls and serve.

Nutrition facts per serving: calories 110, fat 1, fiber 5, carbs 7, protein 5

Peas Salsa

Prep time: 10 minutes I **Cooking time:** 0 minutes I **Servings:** 4

Ingredients:
- 1 cup cherry tomatoes, halved
- 2 cups snow peas, steamed and cooled
- 1 tablespoon lemon juice
- 2 garlic cloves, minced
- 1 avocado, peeled, pitted and cubed
- 1 tablespoon olive oil
- 1 tablespoon cilantro, chopped
- A pinch of cayenne pepper

Directions:
1. In a bowl, mix the cherry tomatoes with the peas and the other ingredients, toss well, divide into smaller bowls and serve.

Nutrition facts per serving: calories 120, fat 2, fiber 4, carbs 6, protein 6

Nutmeg Apple Chips

Prep time: 10 minutes I **Cooking time:** 1 hour I **Servings:** 4

Ingredients:
- Cooking spray
- 2 apples, cored thinly sliced
- 1 tablespoon cinnamon powder
- A pinch of nutmeg, ground

Directions:
1. Arrange the apples on a lined baking sheet, add the other ingredients, toss and cook at 360 degrees F for 1 hour.
2. Divide into bowls and serve as a snack

Nutrition facts per serving: calories 141, fat 2, fiber 2, carbs 7, protein 5

Cucumber Spread

Prep time: 10 minutes I **Cooking time:** 0 minutes I **Servings:** 4

Ingredients:
- 2 cups coconut cream
- 2 cucumbers, chopped
- 1 tablespoon dill, chopped
- 2 teaspoons thyme, dried
- 2 teaspoons parsley, dried
- 2 teaspoons chives, chopped
- A pinch of sea salt and black pepper

Directions:
1. In a blender, combine the cream with the cucumbers and the other ingredients, pulse, divide into bowls and serve cold.

Nutrition facts per serving: calories 120, fat 3, fiber 5, carbs 5, protein 3

Beans, Cucumber and Tomato Salsa

Prep time: 15 minutes I **Cooking time:** 0 minutes I **Servings:** 6

Ingredients:
- 1 cup garbanzo beans, cooked
- 1 cup black beans, cooked
- ½ cup cherry tomatoes, cubed
- 1 cucumber, cubed
- 2 tablespoons lime juice
- 1 tablespoon olive oil
- 5 garlic cloves, minced
- ½ teaspoon cumin, ground
- A pinch of salt and black pepper

Directions:
1. In a bowl, combine the beans with the tomatoes, cucumber and the other ingredients, toss well and serve cold as a snack.

Nutrition facts per serving: calories 170, fat 3, fiber 7, carbs 10, protein 8

Bell Peppers Cakes

Prep time: 10 minutes I **Cooking time:** 10 minutes I **Servings:** 6

Ingredients:
- 1 tablespoon olive oil
- ½ cup cilantro, chopped
- 2 spring onions, chopped
- 1 red bell pepper, chopped
- 1 green bell pepper, chopped
- 1 egg
- ½ cup almond flour
- A pinch of salt and black pepper
- 2 garlic cloves, minced
- 3 zucchinis, grated

Directions:
1. In a bowl, combine the zucchinis with the bell peppers and the other ingredients except the oil, stir well and shape medium patties out of this mix.
2. Heat up a pan with the oil over medium heat, add the patties, cook for 5 minutes on each side, arrange on a platter and serve.

Nutrition facts per serving: calories 120, fat 4, fiber 2, carbs 6, protein 6

Italian Broccoli Bowls

Prep time: 10 minutes I **Cooking time:** 25 minutes I **Servings:** 4

Ingredients:
- 1 pound broccoli florets
- Cooking spray
- 2 eggs, whisked
- 1 teaspoon Italian seasoning
- A pinch of sea salt and black pepper
- 1 teaspoon smoked paprika
- 1 teaspoon cumin, ground

Directions:
1. In a bowl, mix the eggs with the Italian seasoning and the other ingredients except the broccoli and the cooking spray and whisk well.
2. Dip the broccoli florets in the eggs mix, arrange them on a baking sheet lined with parchment paper, grease them with cooking spray and bake at 380 degrees F for 25 minutes.
3. Divide the broccoli bites into bowls and serve.

Nutrition facts per serving: calories 120, fat 6, fiber 2, carbs 6, protein 7

Mushrooms Bowls

Prep time: 10 minutes I **Cooking time:** 25 minutes I **Servings:** 6

Ingredients:
- 2 pound brown mushroom caps
- 1 tablespoon olive oil
- A pinch of sea salt and black pepper
- 1 tablespoon balsamic vinegar
- 1 tablespoon chives, chopped
- 1 teaspoon sweet paprika

Directions:
1. Arrange mushroom caps on a baking sheet lined with parchment paper, add the oil, salt, pepper and the other ingredients, toss well and bake at 390 degrees F for 25 minutes.
2. Divide the mushroom caps in bowls and serve.

Nutrition facts per serving: calories 120, fat 2, fiber 2, carbs 6, protein 5

Artichoke Spread

Prep time: 10 minutes I **Cooking time:** 35 minutes I **Servings:** 8

Ingredients:
- ½ cup almond milk
- 1 cup coconut cream
- 10 ounces artichoke hearts, chopped
- 4 garlic cloves, minced
- A pinch of black pepper
- 1 tablespoon oregano, dried

Directions:
1. In a pan, combine the cream with the almond milk and the other ingredients, toss, bring to a simmer and cook over medium heat for 35 minutes.
2. Blend the mix using an immersion blender, divide into bowls and serve as a party dip.

Nutrition facts per serving: calories 130, fat 5, fiber 4, carbs 6, protein 6

Ginger Pineapple Snack

Prep time: 10 minutes I **Cooking time:** 20 minutes I **Servings:** 6

Ingredients:
- 14 ounces pineapple, cubed
- ½ teaspoon ginger, grated
- 1 tablespoon balsamic vinegar
- ½ teaspoon rosemary, dried
- 1 tablespoon olive oil

Directions:
1. In a bowl, combine the pineapple bites with the ginger and the other ingredients, toss, divide into bowls and serve as a snack.

Nutrition facts per serving: calories 54, fat 2.4, fiber 1, carbs 8.9, protein 0.4

Onions Bowls

Prep time: 10 minutes I **Cooking time:** 12 minutes I **Servings:** 4

Ingredients:
- 2 cups pearl onions, peeled
- Juice of 1 lime
- 1 tablespoon olive oil
- 1 tablespoon ginger, grated
- 1 teaspoon turmeric powder
- 1 small parsley bunch, chopped
- A pinch of salt and black pepper

Directions:
1. Heat up a pan with the oil over medium-high heat, add the pearl onions, lime juice and the other ingredients, toss and cook over medium heat for 12 minutes.
2. Divide the mix into bowls and serve as a snack.

Nutrition facts per serving: calories 135, fat 2, fiber 4, carbs 9, protein 12

Ginger Clams

Prep time: 10 minutes I **Cooking time:** 12 minutes I **Servings:** 4

Ingredients:
- 1 pound clams, scrubbed
- 3 garlic cloves, minced
- 1 tablespoon olive oil
- 1 teaspoon ginger, grated
- 1 teaspoon chili powder
- A pinch of sweet paprika
- ½ cup chicken stock

Directions:
1. Heat up a pan with the oil over medium heat, add the garlic and the ginger and sauté for 2 minutes.
2. Add the clams and the other ingredients, toss, bring to a simmer and cook over medium heat for 10 minutes.
3. Arrange the clams on a platter and serve.

Nutrition facts per serving: calories 93, fat 4, fiber 0.8, carbs 14, protein 1

Dill Tuna Bites

Prep time: 10 minutes I **Cooking time:** 12 minutes I **Servings:** 6

Ingredients:
- 1 pound tuna fillets, boneless and cut into cubes
- 2 teaspoons dill, chopped
- 2 tablespoons olive oil
- 1 teaspoon garlic powder
- Salt and black pepper to the taste
- 2 tablespoon chives, chopped
- 1 tablespoon mustard

Directions:
1. In a bowl, mix the tuna with the dill, oil and the other ingredients except the chives, toss well and arrange on a baking sheet lined with parchment paper.
2. Bake the tuna bites at 400 degrees F for 12 minutes, divide into small bowls, sprinkle the chives on top and serve.

Nutrition facts per serving: calories 140, fat 2, fiber 5, carbs 7, protein 6

Green Chips

Prep time: 10 minutes I **Cooking time:** 15 minutes I **Servings:** 4

Ingredients:
- 2 tablespoons olive oil
- 1 pound kale leaves, pat dried
- 2 tablespoons garlic, minced
- 1 tablespoon lemon zest, grated
- Salt and black pepper to the taste

Directions:
1. Spread the kale leaves on a baking sheet lined with parchment paper, add the oil and the other ingredients, toss a bit and cook in the oven at 400 degrees F for 15 minutes.
2. Cool the kale chips down, divide into bowls and serve as a snack.

Nutrition facts per serving: calories 149, fat 4, fiber 3, carbs 9, protein 6

Peppers and Cilantro Salsa

Prep time: 10 minutes I **Cooking time:** 0 minutes I **Servings:** 4

Ingredients:
- 1 pound mixed bell peppers, cut into strips
- 1 cup cherry tomatoes, cubed
- 1 cucumber, cubed
- 1 avocado, peeled, pitted and cubed
- Salt and black pepper to the taste
- 1 tablespoon olive oil
- ½ cup cilantro, chopped
- 1 tablespoon garlic, minced
- ½ cup green onion, chopped
- 1 tablespoon lemon juice

Directions:
1. In a bowl, combine the bell peppers with the tomatoes, cucumber, the avocado and the other ingredients, toss well, divide into small bowls and serve cold as a snack.

Nutrition facts per serving: calories 170, fat 13.6, fiber 5.1, carbs 12.8, protein 2.6

Shrimp Bowls

Prep time: 10 minutes Cooking time: **0 minutes** Servings: **4**

Ingredients:
- 1 pound shrimp, peeled, deveined, and cooked
- 1 cup kalamata olives, pitted and sliced
- 1 cup cherry tomatoes, cubed
- ½ cup basil, chopped
- A pinch of salt and black pepper
- 2 tablespoons lime juice
- 2 teaspoons chili powder

Directions:
1. In a bowl, combine the shrimp with the kalamata, tomatoes and the other ingredients, toss well, divide into smaller bowls and serve.

Nutrition facts per serving: calories 186, fat 5.8, fiber 2.1, carbs 6.4, protein 26.8

Italian Salmon Bowls

Prep time: 10 minutes I **Cooking time:** 14 minutes I **Servings:** 4

Ingredients:
- 1 pound salmon fillets, boneless and cubed
- 2 tablespoons olive oil
- 1 teaspoon Italian seasoning
- 1 teaspoon garlic, minced
- ½ cup kalamata olives, pitted and chopped
- ¼ cup basil, chopped
- Salt and black pepper to the taste

Directions:
1. In a bowl, combine the salmon with the oil, the Italian seasoning and the other ingredients, toss, arrange on a baking sheet lined with parchment paper and cook at 400 degrees F for 14 minutes.
2. Divide the salmon into bowls and serve.

Nutrition facts per serving: calories 270, fat 7.5, fiber 2, carbs 7, protein 7

Avocado and Olives Salsa

Prep time: 10 minutes I **Cooking time:** 0 minutes I **Servings:** 4

Ingredients:
- 2 avocados, peeled, pitted and roughly cubed
- 2 tablespoons olive oil
- 1 cup kalamata olives, pitted and halved
- ½ cup cherry tomatoes, cubed
- Juice of 1 lime
- Salt and black pepper to the taste
- 1 tablespoon basil, chopped

Directions:
1. In a bowl, combine the avocados with the lime juice and the other ingredients, toss, divide into small bowls and serve as a snack.

Nutrition facts per serving: calories 180, fat 3, fiber 5, carbs 8, protein 6

Seafood Bowls

Prep time: 5 minutes I **Cooking time:** 10 minutes I **Servings:** 4

Ingredients:
- 1 pound mussels, debearded and scrubbed
- ½ pound shrimp, peeled and deveined
- 4 scallions, chopped
- 2 garlic cloves, minced
- 1 tablespoon olive oil
- 1 tablespoon lemon juice

Directions:
1. Heat up a pan with the oil over medium heat, add the scallions and the garlic and sauté for 2 minutes.
2. Add the rest of the ingredients, toss, cook over medium heat for 8 minutes more, divide into bowls and serve.

Nutrition facts per serving: calories 90, fat 4, fiber 5, carbs 5, protein 2

Cayenne Calamari Bites

Prep time: 10 minutes I **Cooking time:** 20 minutes I **Servings:** 4

Ingredients:
- 1 pound calamari rings
- 2 tablespoons olive oil
- ½ cup chicken stock
- A pinch of cayenne pepper
- A pinch of salt and black pepper
- 1 tablespoons lemon juice
- 1 teaspoon chili powder
- 1 teaspoon cumin, ground
- 1 tablespoon chives, chopped

Directions:
1. Heat up a pan with the oil over medium heat, add the calamari, the stock and the other ingredients, toss, cook for 20 minutes, divide into small bowls and serve.

Nutrition facts per serving: calories 155, fat 8, fiber 3, carbs 3, protein 7

Turmeric Seafood Mix

Prep time: 10 minutes I **Cooking time:** 12 minutes I **Servings:** 4

Ingredients:
- 1 cup calamari rings
- 1 cup clams, scrubbed
- 1 pound shrimp, peeled and deveined
- 1 tablespoon avocado oil
- 1 teaspoon lemon juice
- ½ teaspoon rosemary, dried
- 1 teaspoon chili powder
- ½ cup chicken stock
- Salt and black pepper to the taste
- ½ teaspoon turmeric powder

Directions:
1. Heat up a pan with the oil over medium heat, add the shrimp, the calamari rings, the clams and the other ingredients, toss, cook for 12 minutes, arrange on a platter and serve.

Nutrition facts per serving: calories 238, fat 8, fiber 3, carbs 10, protein 8

Coconut Celery Spread

Prep time: 10 minutes I **Cooking time:** 15 minutes I **Servings:** 4

Ingredients:
- 4 celery stalks
- 3 scallions, chopped
- 1 tablespoon olive oil
- 1 tablespoon lime juice
- ½ teaspoon chili powder
- 1 cup coconut cream
- Salt and black pepper to the taste
- 2 tablespoons parsley, chopped

Directions:
1. Heat up a pan with the oil over medium heat, add the scallions and sauté for 2 minutes.
2. Add the celery and the other ingredients, toss, cook over medium heat for 13 minutes more, blend using an immersion blender, divide into bowls and serve s a snack.

Nutrition facts per serving: calories 140, fat 10, fiber 3, carbs 6, protein 13

Creamy Coconut Shrimp

Prep time: 5 minutes I **Cooking time:** 10 minutes I **Servings:** 4

Ingredients:
- 1 pound shrimp, peeled and deveined
- 2 shallots, chopped
- 1 tablespoon olive oil
- Salt and black pepper to the taste
- 1 teaspoon rosemary, dried
- 2 cups coconut cream
- 1 cup cilantro, chopped

Directions:
1. Heat up a pan with the oil over medium heat, add the shallots and sauté for 2 minutes.
2. Add the shrimp and the other ingredients, toss, cook over medium heat for 8 minutes, divide into bowls and serve.

Nutrition facts per serving: calories 220, fat 8, fiber 0, carbs 5, protein 12

Herbed Salsa

Prep time: 10 minutes I **Cooking time:** 0 minutes I **Servings:** 4

Ingredients:
- 2 tablespoons olive oil
- 2 fennel bulbs, shredded
- 1 cup kalamata olives, pitted and halved
- 1 tablespoon balsamic vinegar
- A pinch of salt and black pepper
- 2 tablespoons lime juice
- 2 tablespoons parsley, chopped
- 2 tablespoons mint, chopped

Directions:
1. In a bowl, mix the fennel with the oil and the other ingredients, toss well, keep in the fridge for 10 minutes, divide into bowls and serve.

Nutrition facts per serving: calories 160, fat 7, fiber 2, carbs 7, protein 8

Mango Salsa

Prep time: 10 minutes I **Cooking time:** 0 minutes I **Servings:** 4

Ingredients:
- 2 mangoes, peeled and cubed
- 2 oranges, peeled and cut into segments
- ½ cup kalamata olives, pitted and halved
- Juice of 1 orange
- Zest of 1 orange, grated
- Juice of 1 lime
- 2 red chili peppers, chopped
- ½ teaspoon ginger, grated
- A pinch of salt and black pepper
- 1 tablespoon avocado oil
- ¼ cup cilantro, chopped

Directions:
1. In a bowl, mix the mangoes with the oranges and the other ingredients, toss, divide into smaller bowls and serve.

Nutrition facts per serving: calories 170, fat 3, fiber 5.7, carbs 37.6, protein 2.5

Salmon and Cucumber Wraps

Prep time: 10 minutes I **Cooking time:** 0 minutes I **Servings:** 4

Ingredients:
- 6 ounces smoked salmon, skinless and thinly sliced
- 1 red bell pepper, cut into strips
- 1 cucumber, cut into strips
- 2 tablespoons coconut cream

Directions:
1. Place the smoked salmon slices on a working surface, spread the coconut cream on each, divide the cucumber and the bell pepper strips on each slide, roll and serve as a snack.

Nutrition facts per serving: calories 120, fat 6, fiber 6, carbs 12, protein 6

Garlic Mussels and Quinoa

Prep time: 10 minutes I **Cooking time:** 12 minutes I **Servings:** 4

Ingredients:
- 1 pound mussels, scrubbed
- 2 cups quinoa, cooked
- ½ cup chicken soup
- 1 teaspoon red pepper flakes, crushed
- 1 teaspoon hot paprika
- 2 garlic cloves, minced
- 2 tablespoons parsley, chopped
- 2 tablespoons avocado oil
- 1 yellow onion, chopped
- A pinch of salt and black pepper

Directions:
1. Heat up a pan with the oil over medium heat, add the onion and the garlic and sauté for 2 minutes.
2. Add the mussels, quinoa and the other ingredients, toss, cook over medium heat for 10 minutes more, divide into small bowls and serve.

Nutrition facts per serving: calories 150, fat 3, fiber 3, carbs 6, protein 8

Tuna Bites

Prep time: 10 minutes I **Cooking time:** 10 minutes I **Servings:** 4

Ingredients:
- 1 pound tuna fillets, boneless, skinless and cubed
- 2 tablespoons olive oil
- 4 scallions, chopped
- Juice of 1 lime
- 1 teaspoon sweet paprika
- 1 teaspoon turmeric powder
- 2 tablespoons coconut aminos
- A pinch of salt and black pepper

Directions:
1. Heat up a pan with the oil over medium heat, add the scallions and sauté for 2 minutes.
2. Add the tuna bites and cook them for 2 minutes on each side.
3. Add the remaining ingredients, toss gently, cook everything for 4 minutes more, arrange everything on a platter and serve.

Nutrition facts per serving: calories 210, fat 7, fiber 6, carbs 6, protein 7

Berries Salsa

Ingredients:
- 1 pound cherry tomatoes, cubed
- 1 cup blackberries
- ½ cup strawberries
- 2 tablespoons avocado oil
- 4 scallions, chopped
- 2 tablespoons garlic powder
- A pinch of salt and black pepper
- ½ tablespoon mint, chopped
- 1 tablespoon chives, chopped

Directions:
1. In a bowl, combine the tomatoes with the blackberries, strawberries and the other ingredients, toss, divide into small bowls and serve really cold.

Nutrition facts per serving: calories 60, fat 3, fiber 2, carbs 6, protein 7

Tomato Dip

Prep time: 10 minutes I **Cooking time:** 12 minutes I **Servings:** 6

Ingredients:
- 1 pound tomatoes, chopped
- 2 carrots, grated
- 4 ounces coconut cream
- A pinch of salt and black pepper
- 1 teaspoon chili powder
- Cooking spray

Directions:
1. In a pan, combine the tomatoes with the carrots and the other ingredients, toss and cook over medium heat for 12 minutes.
2. Blend using an immersion blender, divide into small bowls and serve as a party dip.

Nutrition facts per serving: calories 150, fat 4, fiber 6, carbs 14, protein 6

Cayenne Avocado Bites

Prep time: 10 minutes I **Cooking time:** 0 minutes I **Servings:** 2

Ingredients:
- 2 avocados, halved, pitted and cubed
- ½ pound shrimp, cooked, peeled and deveined
- A pinch of salt and black pepper
- 1 tablespoon lemon juice
- 2 tablespoons olive oil
- 1 teaspoon cayenne pepper
- ½ teaspoon rosemary, dried
- ½ teaspoon oregano, dried
- 1 teaspoon sweet paprika

Directions:
1. In a bowl, combine the avocados with the shrimp, salt, pepper and the other ingredients, toss, divide into small bowls and serve.

Nutrition facts per serving: calories 160, fat 10, fiber 7, carbs 12, protein 7

Basil Radish Snack

Prep time: 5 minutes I **Cooking time:** 25 minutes I **Servings:** 4

Ingredients:
- 1 pound radishes, cut into wedges
- 2 tablespoons olive oil
- ½ teaspoon garam masala
- ½ teaspoon oregano, dried
- ½ teaspoon basil, dried
- Salt and black pepper to the taste
- 1 tablespoon chives, chopped

Directions:
1. Spread the radishes on a baking sheet lined with parchment paper, add the oil, garam masala and the other ingredients, toss and bake at 420 degrees F for 25 minutes.
2. Divide the radish bites into bowls and serve as a snack.

Nutrition facts per serving: calories 30, fat 1, fiber 2, carbs 7, protein 1

Radish Dip

Prep time: 5 minutes I **Cooking time:** 0 minutes I **Servings:** 4

Ingredients:
- 2 avocados, pitted, peeled and chopped
- 1 cup radishes, chopped
- 1 cup coconut cream
- 4 spring onions, chopped
- 1 tablespoon lemon juice
- A pinch of salt and black pepper
- 1 tablespoon avocado oil

Directions:
1. In a blender, combine the avocados with the radishes and the other ingredients, pulse well, divide into bowls and serve as a party dip.

Nutrition facts per serving: calories 162, fat 8, fiber 4, carbs 6, protein 6

Ginger Olives Salsa

Prep time: 10 minutes I **Cooking time:** 0 minutes I **Servings:** 6

Ingredients:
- 1 teaspoon cumin seeds
- 1 tablespoon avocado oil
- 2 oranges, peeled and cut into segments
- 1 cup kalamata olives, pitted and halved
- 1 tablespoon oregano, chopped
- 1 tablespoon chives, chopped
- 1 tablespoon balsamic vinegar
- ½ tablespoon ginger, grated
- ½ teaspoon fennel seeds

Directions:
1. In a bowl, combine the oranges with the olives, cumin and the other ingredients, toss, keep in the fridge for 10 minutes, divide into small bowls and serve.

Nutrition facts per serving: calories 120, fat 1, fiber 3, carbs 5, protein 9

Basil Peppers Salsa

Prep time: 5 minutes I **Cooking time:** 0 minutes I **Servings:** 4

Ingredients:
- 1 tablespoon olive oil
- 2 red bell peppers, cut into thin strips
- 2 green bell peppers, cut into strips
- 1 cup radishes, cubed
- 2 tablespoons balsamic vinegar
- 1 tablespoon ginger, grated
- 1 teaspoon chili powder
- 1 tablespoon lemon juice
- A pinch of salt and black pepper
- 1 tablespoon basil, chopped

Directions:
1. In a bowl, combine the bell peppers with the radishes, the oil and the other ingredients, toss, divide into small bowls and serve as a party salsa.

Nutrition facts per serving: calories 107, fat 4, fiber 2, carbs 6, protein 6

Beans Dip

Prep time: 10 minutes I **Cooking time:** 20 minutes I **Servings:** 6

Ingredients:
- 2 cups red kidney beans, cooked
- 2 tablespoons olive oil
- 1 yellow onion, chopped
- ½ cup chicken stock
- ½ cup coconut cream
- ¼ teaspoon oregano, dried
- ¼ teaspoon garlic powder
- ¼ teaspoon onion powder
- Salt and black pepper to the taste
- 1 tablespoon chives, chopped

Directions:
1. Heat up a pan with the oil over medium heat, add the onion and sauté for 5 minutes.
2. Add the stock, oregano and the other ingredients except the cream and the chives, stir, and cook over medium heat for 15 minutes more.
3. Add the cream, blend the mix using an immersion blender, divide into bowls and serve with the chives sprinkled on top.

Nutrition facts per serving: calories 302, fat 10.2, fiber 10.2, carbs 40.7, protein 14.6

Mint Dip

Prep time: 10 minutes I **Cooking time:** 0 minutes I **Servings:** 4

Ingredients:
- 2 avocados, pitted, peeled and chopped
- 1 cup cherry tomatoes, chopped
- 1 tablespoon lemon juice
- 2 tablespoons coconut oil
- 1 teaspoon chili powder
- ½ cup mint, chopped
- A pinch of salt and black pepper

Directions:
1. In a blender, mix the tomatoes with the avocado and the other ingredients, pulse well, divide into small bowls and serve as a party dip.

Nutrition facts per serving: calories 150, fat 7, fiber 6, carbs 8.8, protein 6

Shrimp and Watermelon Bowls

Prep time: 10 minutes I **Cooking time:** 0 minutes I **Servings:** 4

Ingredients:
- 2 tablespoons avocado oil
- 4 scallions, chopped
- 1 pound shrimp, cooked, deveined and peeled
- 1 cup watermelon, peeled and cubed
- ½ cup strawberries
- 2 tablespoons lemon juice
- A pinch of cayenne pepper
- 1 tablespoon balsamic vinegar

Directions:
1. In a bowl, combine the shrimp with the watermelon, scallions and the other ingredients, toss, divide into smaller bowls and serve.

Nutrition facts per serving: calories 205, fat 12, fiber 2, carbs 9, protein 8

Cayenne Dip

Prep time: 10 minutes I **Cooking time:** 0 minutes I **Servings:** 4

Ingredients:
- 1 avocado, pitted, peeled and chopped
- 1 red chili pepper, minced
- 1 cup blackberries
- ½ cup blueberries
- A pinch of cayenne pepper
- 2 tablespoons lemon juice

Directions:
1. In a blender, combine the avocado with the berries and the other ingredients, pulse well, divide into small bowls and serve as a party dip.

Nutrition facts per serving: calories 120, fat 2, fiber 2, carbs 7, protein 4

Lemon Triangles

Prep time: 5 minutes I **Cooking time:** 25 minutes I **Servings:** 4

Ingredients:
- 1 cup coconut flour
- A pinch of salt and black pepper
- 1 cup cilantro, chopped
- 1 teaspoon lemon zest, grated
- 1 tablespoon lemon juice
- 2 eggs, whisked
- ½ teaspoon baking powder

Directions:
1. In a bowl, mix the flour with the eggs and the other ingredients, and stir well.
2. Spread the mix on a baking sheet lined with parchment paper, cut into triangles and cook at 380 degrees F for 25 minutes.
3. Cool the squares down and serve them as a snack.

Nutrition facts per serving: calories 49, fat 2.7, fiber 1.4, carbs 2.8, protein 3.4

Coconut Peppers Spread

Prep time: 4 minutes I **Cooking time:** 0 minutes I **Servings:** 4

Ingredients:
- 1 teaspoon turmeric powder
- 1 cup coconut cream
- 14 ounces red peppers, chopped
- Juice of ½ lemon
- 1 tablespoon chives, chopped

Directions:
1. In your blender, combine the peppers with the turmeric and the other ingredients except the chives, pulse well, divide into bowls and serve as a snack with the chives sprinkled on top.

Nutrition facts per serving: calories 183, fat 14.9, fiber 3. carbs 12.7, protein 3.4

Lentils Cilantro Dip

Prep time: 5 minutes I **Cooking time:** 0 minutes I **Servings:** 4

Ingredients:
- 14 ounces lentils, cooked
- Juice of 1 lemon
- 2 garlic cloves, minced
- 2 tablespoons olive oil
- ½ cup cilantro, chopped

Directions:
1. In a blender, combine the lentils with the oil and the other ingredients, pulse well, divide into bowls and serve as a party spread.

Nutrition facts per serving: calories 416, fat 8.2, fiber 30.4, carbs 60.4, protein 25.8

Spiced Walnuts Mix

Prep time: 5 minutes I **Cooking time:** 15 minutes I **Servings:** 8

Ingredients:
- ½ teaspoon smoked paprika
- ½ teaspoon chili powder
- ½ teaspoon garlic powder
- 1 tablespoon avocado oil
- A pinch of cayenne pepper
- 14 ounces walnuts

Directions:
1. Spread the walnuts on a lined baking sheet, add the paprika and the other ingredients, toss and bake at 410 degrees F for 15 minutes.
2. Divide into bowls and serve as a snack.

Nutrition facts per serving: calories 311, fat 29.6, fiber 3.6, carbs 5.3, protein 12

Cranberry Bites

Prep time: 3 hours and 5 minutes I **Cooking time:** 0 minutes I **Servings:** 4

Ingredients:
- 2 ounces coconut cream
- 2 tablespoons rolled oats
- 2 tablespoons coconut, shredded
- 1 cup cranberries

Directions:
1. In a blender, combine the oats with the cranberries and the other ingredients, pulse well and spread into a square pan.
2. Cut into squares and keep them in the fridge for 3 hours before serving.

Nutrition facts per serving: calories 66, fat 4.4, fiber 1.8, carbs 5.4, protein 0.8

Cheddar Cauliflower Bars

Prep time: 10 minutes I **Cooking time:** 30 minutes I **Servings:** 8

Ingredients:
- 2 cups whole wheat flour
- 2 teaspoons baking powder
- A pinch of black pepper
- 2 eggs, whisked
- 1 cup almond milk
- 1 cup cauliflower florets, chopped
- ½ cup cheddar, shredded

Directions:
1. In a bowl, combine the flour with the cauliflower and the other ingredients and stir well.
2. Spread into a baking tray, introduce in the oven, bake at 400 degrees F for 30 minutes, cut into bars and serve as a snack.

Nutrition facts per serving: calories 430, fat 18.1, fiber 3.7, carbs 54, protein 14.5

Almonds Bowls

Prep time: 5 minutes I **Cooking time:** 10 minutes I **Servings:** 4

Ingredients:
- 2 cups almonds
- ¼ cup coconut, shredded
- 1 mango, peeled and cubed
- 1 cup sunflower seeds
- Cooking spray

Directions:
1. Spread the almonds, coconut, mango and sunflower seeds on a baking tray, grease with the cooking spray, toss and bake at 400 degrees F for 10 minutes.
2. Divide into bowls and serve as a snack.

Nutrition facts per serving: calories 411, fat 31.8, fiber 8.7, carbs 25.8, protein 13.3

Paprika Potato Chips

Prep time: 10 minutes I **Cooking time:** 20 minutes I **Servings:** 4

Ingredients:
- 4 gold potatoes, peeled and thinly sliced
- 2 tablespoons olive oil
- 1 tablespoon chili powder
- 1 teaspoon sweet paprika
- 1 tablespoon chives, chopped

Directions:
1. Spread the chips on a lined baking sheet, add the oil and the other ingredients, toss, introduce in the oven and bake at 390 degrees F for 20 minutes.
2. Divide into bowls and serve.

Nutrition facts per serving: calories 118, fat 7.4, fiber 2.9, carbs 13.4, protein 1.3

Kale Spread

Prep time: 10 minutes I **Cooking time:** 20 minutes I **Servings:** 4

Ingredients:
- 1 bunch kale leaves
- 1 cup coconut cream
- 1 shallot, chopped
- 1 tablespoon olive oil
- 1 teaspoon chili powder
- A pinch of black pepper

Directions:
1. Heat up a pan with the oil over medium heat, add the shallots, stir and sauté for 4 minutes.
2. Add the kale and the other ingredients, bring to a simmer and cook over medium heat for 16 minutes.
3. Blend using an immersion blender, divide into bowls and serve as a snack.

Nutrition facts per serving: calories 188, fat 17.9, fiber 2.1, carbs 7.6, protein 2.5

Garlic Beets Bites

Prep time: 10 minutes I **Cooking time:** 35 minutes I **Servings:** 4

Ingredients:
- 2 beets, peeled and thinly sliced
- 1 tablespoon avocado oil
- 1 teaspoon cumin, ground
- 1 teaspoon fennel seeds, crushed
- 2 teaspoons garlic, minced

Directions:
1. Spread the beet chips on a lined baking sheet, add the oil and the other ingredients, toss, introduce in the oven and bake at 400 degrees F for 35 minutes.
2. Divide into bowls and serve as a snack.

Nutrition facts per serving: calories 32, fat 0.7, fiber 1.4, carbs 6.1, protein 1.1

Yogurt Zucchini Dip

Prep time: 5 minutes I **Cooking time:** 10 minutes I **Servings:** 4

Ingredients:
- ½ cup nonfat yogurt
- 2 zucchinis, chopped
- 1 tablespoon olive oil
- 2 spring onions, chopped
- ¼ cup veggie stock
- 2 garlic cloves, minced
- 1 tablespoon dill, chopped
- A pinch of nutmeg, ground

Directions:
1. Heat up a pan with the oil over medium heat, add the onions and garlic, stir and sauté for 3 minutes.
2. Add the zucchinis and the other ingredients except the yogurt, toss, cook for 7 minutes more and take off the heat.
3. Add the yogurt, blend using an immersion blender, divide into bowls and serve.

Nutrition facts per serving: calories 76, fat 4.1, fiber 1.5, carbs 7.2, protein 3.4

Apple Bites

Prep time: 10 minutes I **Cooking time:** 20 minutes I **Servings:** 4

Ingredients:
- 2 tablespoons olive oil
- 1 teaspoon smoked paprika
- 1 cup sunflower seeds
- 1 cup chia seeds
- 2 apples, cored and cut into wedges
- ½ teaspoon cumin, ground
- A pinch of cayenne pepper

Directions:
1. In a bowl, combine the seeds with the apples and the other ingredients, toss, spread on a lined baking sheet, introduce in the oven and bake at 350 degrees F for 20 minutes.
2. Divide into bowls and serve as a snack.

Nutrition facts per serving: calories 222, fat 15.4, fiber 6.4, carbs 21.1, protein 4

Pumpkin and Lemon Dip

Prep time: 5 minutes I **Cooking time:** 0 minutes I **Servings:** 4

Ingredients:
- 2 cups pumpkin flesh
- ½ cup pumpkin seeds
- 1 tablespoon lemon juice
- 1 tablespoon sesame seed paste
- 1 tablespoon olive oil

Directions:
1. In a blender, combine the pumpkin with the seeds and the other ingredients, pulse well, divide into bowls and serve a party spread.

Nutrition facts per serving: calories 162, fat 12.7, fiber 2.3, carbs 9.7, protein 5.5

Dill Spinach Spread

Prep time: 10 minutes I **Cooking time:** 20 minutes I **Servings:** 4

Ingredients:
- 1 pound spinach, chopped
- 1 cup coconut cream
- 1 cup mozzarella, shredded
- A pinch of black pepper
- 1 tablespoon dill, chopped

Directions:
1. In a baking pan, combine the spinach with the cream and the other ingredients, stir well, introduce in the oven and bake at 400 degrees F for 20 minutes.
2. Divide into bowls and serve.

Nutrition facts per serving: calories 186, fat 14.8, fiber 4.4, carbs 8.4, protein 8.8

Cilantro Salsa

Prep time: 5 minutes I **Cooking time:** 0 minutes I **Servings:** 4

Ingredients:
- 1 red onion, chopped
- 1 cup black olives, pitted and halved
- 1 cucumber, cubed
- ¼ cup cilantro, chopped
- A pinch of black pepper
- 2 tablespoons lime juice

Directions:
1. In a bowl, combine the olives with the cucumber and the rest of the ingredients, toss and serve cold as a snack.

Nutrition facts per serving: calories 64, fat 3.7, fiber 2.1, carbs 8.4, protein 1.1

Beets Dip

Prep time: 5 minutes I **Cooking time:** 25 minutes I **Servings:** 4

Ingredients:
- 2 tablespoons olive oil
- 1 red onion, chopped
- 2 tablespoons chives, chopped
- A pinch of black pepper
- 1 beet, peeled and chopped
- 8 ounces cream cheese
- 1 cup coconut cream

Directions:
1. Heat up a pan with the oil over medium heat, add the onion and sauté for 5 minutes.
2. Add the rest of the ingredients, and cook everything for 20 minutes more stirring often.
3. Transfer the mix to a blender, pulse well, divide into bowls and serve.

Nutrition facts per serving: calories 418, fat 41.2, fiber 2.5, carbs 10, protein 6.4

Balsamic Cucumber Bowls

Prep time: 5 minutes I **Cooking time:** 0 minutes I **Servings:** 4

Ingredients:
- 1 pound cucumbers cubed
- 1 avocado, peeled, pitted and cubed
- 1 tablespoon capers, drained
- 1 tablespoon chives, chopped
- 1 small red onion, cubed
- 1 tablespoon olive oil
- 1 tablespoon balsamic vinegar

Directions:
1. In a bowl, combine the cucumbers with the avocado and the other ingredients, toss, divide into small cups and serve.

Nutrition facts per serving: calories 132, fat 4.4, fiber 4, carbs 11.6, protein 4.5

Lemon Chives Chickpeas Dip

Prep time: 5 minutes I **Cooking time:** 0 minutes I **Servings:** 4

Ingredients:
- 1 tablespoon olive oil
- 1 tablespoon lemon juice
- 1 tablespoon sesame seeds paste
- 2 tablespoons chives, chopped
- 2 spring onions, chopped
- 2 cups chickpeas, cooked

Directions:
1. In your blender, combine the chickpeas with the oil and the other ingredients except the chives, pulse well, divide into bowls, sprinkle the chives on top and serve.

Nutrition facts per serving: calories 280, fat 13.3, fiber 5.5, carbs 14.8, protein 6.2

Creamy Olives Spread

Prep time: 4 minutes I **Cooking time:** 0 minutes I **Servings:** 4

Ingredients:
- 2 cups black olives, pitted and chopped
- 1 cup mint, chopped
- 2 tablespoons avocado oil
- ½ cup coconut cream
- ¼ cup lime juice
- A pinch of black pepper

Directions:
1. In your blender, combine the olives with the mint and the other ingredients, pulse well, divide into bowls and serve.

Nutrition facts per serving: calories 287, fat 13.3, fiber 4.7, carbs 17.4, protein 2.4

Onions Dip

Prep time: 5 minutes I **Cooking time:** 0 minutes I **Servings:** 4

Ingredients:
- 4 spring onions, chopped
- 1 shallot, minced
- 1 tablespoon lime juice
- A pinch of black pepper
- 2 ounces mozzarella cheese, shredded
- 1 cup coconut cream
- 1 tablespoon parsley, chopped

Directions:
1. In a blender, combine the spring onions with the shallot and the other ingredients, pulse well, divide into bowls and serve as a party dip.

Nutrition facts per serving: calories 271, fat 15.3, fiber 5, carbs 15.9, protein 6.9

Pine Nuts Dip

Prep time: 5 minutes I **Cooking time:** 0 minutes I **Servings:** 4

Ingredients:
- 8 ounces coconut cream
- 1 tablespoon pine nuts, chopped
- 2 tablespoons parsley, chopped
- A pinch of black pepper

Directions:
1. In a bowl, combine the cream with the pine nuts and the rest of the ingredients, whisk well, divide into bowls and serve.

Nutrition facts per serving: calories 281, fat 13, fiber 4.8, carbs 16, protein 3.56

Arugula Salsa

Prep time: 5 minutes I **Cooking time:** 0 minutes I **Servings:** 4

Ingredients:
- 4 scallions, chopped
- 2 tomatoes, cubed
- 4 cucumbers, cubed
- 1 tablespoon balsamic vinegar
- 1 cup baby arugula leaves
- 2 tablespoons lemon juice
- 2 tablespoons olive oil
- A pinch of black pepper

Directions:
1. In a bowl, combine the scallions with the tomatoes and the other ingredients, toss, divide into small bowls and serve as a snack.

Nutrition facts per serving: calories 139, fat 3.8, fiber 4.5, carbs 14, protein 5.4

Creamy Cheese Spread

Prep time: 5 minutes **Cooking time:** 0 minutes **Servings:** 6

Ingredients:
- 1 tablespoon mint, chopped
- 1 tablespoon oregano, chopped
- 10 ounces cream cheese
- ½ cup ginger, sliced
- 2 tablespoons coconut aminos

Directions:
1. In your blender, combine the cream cheese with the ginger and the other ingredients, pulse well, divide into small cups and serve.

Nutrition facts per serving: calories 388, fat 15.4, fiber 6, carbs 14.3, protein 6

Yogurt Dip

Prep time: 5 minutes I **Cooking time:** 0 minutes I **Servings:** 4

Ingredients:

- 3 cups non-fat yogurt
- 2 spring onions, chopped
- 1 teaspoon sweet paprika
- ¼ cup almonds, chopped
- ¼ cup dill, chopped

Directions:

1. In a bowl, combine the yogurt with the onions and the other ingredients, whisk, divide into bowls and serve.

Nutrition facts per serving: calories 181, fat 12.2, fiber 6, carbs 14,1, protein 7

Cauliflower and Olives Salsa

Prep time: 5 minutes I **Cooking time:** 0 minutes I **Servings:** 4

Ingredients:
- 1 pound cauliflower florets, blanched
- 1 cup kalamata olives, pitted and halved
- 1 cup cherry tomatoes, halved
- 1 tablespoon olive oil
- 1 tablespoon lime juice
- A pinch of black pepper

Directions:
1. In a bowl, combine the cauliflower with the olives and the other ingredients, toss and serve.

Nutrition facts per serving: calories 139, fat 4, fiber 3.6, carbs 5.5, protein 3.4

Shrimp Dip

Prep time: 5 minutes I **Cooking time:** 0 minutes I **Servings:** 4

Ingredients:
- 8 ounces coconut cream
- 1 pound shrimp, cooked, peeled, deveined and chopped
- 2 tablespoons dill, chopped
- 2 spring onions, chopped
- 1 tablespoon cilantro, chopped
- A pinch of black pepper

Directions:
1. In a bowl, combine the shrimp with the cream and the other ingredients, whisk and serve as a party spread.

Nutrition facts per serving: calories 362, fat 14.3, fiber 6, carbs 14.6, protein 5.9

Peach Bowls

Prep time: 4 minutes I **Cooking time:** 0 minutes I **Servings:** 4

Ingredients:
- 4 peaches, stones removed and cubed
- 1 cup kalamata olives, pitted and halved
- 1 avocado, pitted, peeled and cubed
- 1 cup cherry tomatoes, halved
- 1 tablespoon olive oil
- 1 tablespoon lime juice
- 1 tablespoon cilantro, chopped

Directions:
1. In a bowl, combine the peaches with the olives and the other ingredients, toss well and serve cold.

Nutrition facts per serving: calories 200, fat 7.5, fiber 5, carbs 13.3, protein 4.9

Carrot Bites

Prep time: 10 minutes I **Cooking time:** 20 minutes I **Servings:** 4

Ingredients:
- 4 carrots, thinly sliced
- 2 tablespoons olive oil
- A pinch of black pepper
- 1 teaspoon sweet paprika
- ½ teaspoon turmeric powder
- A pinch of red pepper flakes

Directions:
1. In a bowl, combine the carrot chips with the oil and the other ingredients and toss.
2. Spread the chips on a lined baking sheet, bake at 400 degrees F for 25 minutes, divide into bowls and serve as a snack.

Nutrition facts per serving: calories 180, fat 3, fiber 3.3, carbs 5.8, protein 1.3

Asparagus Bites

Prep time: 4 minutes I **Cooking time:** 20 minutes I **Servings:** 4

Ingredients:
- 2 tablespoons coconut oil, melted
- 1 pound asparagus, trimmed and halved
- 1 teaspoon garlic powder
- 1 teaspoon rosemary, dried
- 1 teaspoon chili powder

Directions:
1. In a bowl, mix the asparagus with the oil and the other ingredients, toss, spread on a lined baking sheet and bake at 400 degrees F for 20 minutes.
2. Divide into bowls and serve cold as a snack.

Nutrition facts per serving: calories 170, fat 4.3, fiber 4, carbs 7, protein 4.5

Figs Snack

Prep time: 4 minutes I **Cooking time:** 12 minutes I **Servings:** 4

Ingredients:
- 8 figs, halved
- 1 tablespoon avocado oil
- 1 teaspoon nutmeg, ground

Directions:
1. In a roasting pan combine the figs with the oil and the nutmeg, toss, and bake at 400 degrees F for 12 minutes.
2. Divide the figs into small bowls and serve as a snack.

Nutrition facts per serving: calories 180, fat 4.3, fiber 2, carbs 2, protein 3.2

Cabbage Salsa

Prep time: 5 minutes I **Cooking time:** 6 minutes I **Servings:** 4

Ingredients:
- 2 cups red cabbage, shredded
- 1 pound shrimp, peeled and deveined
- 1 tablespoon olive oil
- A pinch of black pepper
- 2 spring onions, chopped
- 1 cup tomatoes, cubed
- ½ teaspoon garlic powder

Directions:
1. Heat up a pan with the oil over medium heat, add the shrimp, toss and cook for 3 minutes on each side.
2. In a bowl, combine the cabbage with the shrimp and the other ingredients, toss, divide into small bowls and serve.

Nutrition facts per serving: calories 225, fat 9.7, fiber 5.1, carbs 11.4, protein 4.5

Coriander Avocado Wedges

Prep time: 5 minutes I **Cooking time:** 10 minutes I **Servings:** 4

Ingredients:
- 2 avocados, peeled, pitted and cut into wedges
- 1 tablespoon avocado oil
- 1 tablespoon lime juice
- 1 teaspoon coriander, ground

Directions:
1. Spread the avocado wedges on a lined baking sheet, add the oil and the other ingredients, toss, and bake at 300 degrees F for 10 minutes.
2. Divide into cups and serve as a snack.

Nutrition facts per serving: calories 212, fat 20.1, fiber 6.9, carbs 9.8, protein 2

Lemon Dip

Prep time: 4 minutes I **Cooking time:** 0 minutes I **Servings:** 4

Ingredients:
- 1 cup cream cheese
- Black pepper to the taste
- ½ cup lemon juice
- 1 tablespoon cilantro, chopped
- 3 garlic cloves, chopped

Directions:
1. In your food processor, mix the cream cheese with the lemon juice and the other ingredients, pulse well, divide into bowls and serve.

Nutrition facts per serving: calories 213, fat 20.5, fiber 0.2, carbs 2.8, protein 4.8

Coconut Sweet Potato Spread

Prep time: 10 minutes I **Cooking time:** 40 minutes I **Servings:** 4

Ingredients:
- 1 cup sweet potatoes, peeled and cubed
- 1 tablespoon veggie stock
- Cooking spray
- 2 tablespoons coconut cream
- 2 teaspoons rosemary, dried
- Black pepper to the taste

Directions:
1. In a baking pan, combine the potatoes with the stock and the other ingredients, stir, bake at 365 degrees F for 40 minutes, transfer to your blender, pulse well, divide into small bowls and serve

Nutrition facts per serving: calories 65, fat 2.1, fiber 2, carbs 11.3, protein 0.8

Balsamic Salsa

Prep time: 5 minutes I **Cooking time:** 0 minutes I **Servings:** 4

Ingredients:
- 1 cup black beans, cooked
- 1 cup red kidney beans, cooked
- 1 teaspoon balsamic vinegar
- 1 cup cherry tomatoes, cubed
- 1 tablespoon olive oil
- 2 shallots, chopped

Directions:
1. In a bowl, combine the beans with the vinegar and the other ingredients, toss and serve as a party snack.

Nutrition facts per serving: calories 362, fat 4.8, fiber 14.9, carbs 61, protein 21.4

Green Olives Salsa

Ingredients:
- 1 pound green beans, trimmed and halved
- 1 tablespoon olive oil
- 2 teaspoons capers, drained
- 6 ounces green olives, pitted and sliced
- 4 garlic cloves, minced
- 1 tablespoon lime juice
- 1 tablespoon oregano, chopped
- Black pepper to the taste

Directions:
1. Heat up a pan with the oil over medium-high heat, add the garlic and the green beans, toss and cook for 3 minutes.
2. Add the rest of the ingredients, toss, cook for another 7 minutes, divide into small cups and serve cold.

Nutrition facts per serving: calories 111, fat 6.7, fiber 5.6, carbs 13.2, protein 2.9

Carrot and Walnuts Spread

Prep time: 10 minutes I **Cooking time:** 30 minutes I **Servings:** 4

Ingredients:
- 1 pound carrots, peeled and chopped
- ½ cup walnuts, chopped
- 2 cups veggie stock
- 1 cup coconut cream
- 1 tablespoon rosemary, chopped
- 1 teaspoon garlic powder
- ¼ teaspoon smoked paprika

Directions:
1. In a small pot, mix the carrots with the stock, walnuts and the other ingredients except the cream and the rosemary, stir, bring to a boil over medium heat, cook for 30 minutes, drain and transfer to a blender.
2. Add the cream, blend the mix well, divide into bowls, sprinkle the rosemary on top and serve.

Nutrition facts per serving: calories 201, fat 8.7, fiber 3.4, carbs 7.8, protein 7.7

Garlic Tomato Spread

Prep time: 10 minutes I **Cooking time:** 10 minutes I **Servings:** 4

Ingredients:
- 1 pound tomatoes, peeled and chopped
- ½ cup garlic, minced
- 2 tablespoons olive oil
- A pinch of black pepper
- 2 shallots, chopped
- 1 teaspoon thyme, dried

Directions:
1. Heat up a pan with the oil over medium-high heat, add the garlic and the shallots, stir and sauté for 2 minutes.
2. Add the tomatoes and the other ingredients, cook for 8 minutes more and transfer to a blender.
3. Pulse well, divide into small cups and serve as a snack.

Nutrition facts per serving: calories 232, fat 11.3, fiber 3.9, carbs 7.9, protein 4.5

Salmon and Spinach Cups

Prep time: 10 minutes I **Cooking time:** 0 minutes I **Servings:** 6

Ingredients:
- 1 tablespoon avocado oil
- 1 tablespoon balsamic vinegar
- ½ teaspoon oregano, dried
- 1 cup smoked salmon, boneless, skinless and cubed
- 1 cup salsa
- 4 cups baby spinach

Directions:
1. In a bowl, combine the salmon with the salsa and the other ingredients, toss, divide into small cups and serve.

Nutrition facts per serving: calories 281, fat 14.4, fiber 7.4, carbs 18.7, protein 7.4

Corn Salsa

Ingredients:
- 3 cups corn
- 2 cups tomatoes, cubed
- 2 green onions, chopped
- 2 tablespoons olive oil
- 1 red chili pepper, chopped
- ½ tablespoon chives, chopped

Directions:
1. In a salad bowl, combine the tomatoes with the corn and the other ingredients, toss and serve cold as a snack.

Nutrition facts per serving: calories 178, fat 8.6, fiber 4.5, carbs 25.9, protein 4.7

Mushroom Snack

Prep time: 10 minutes I **Cooking time:** 25 minutes I **Servings:** 4

Ingredients:
- 1 pound small mushroom caps
- 2 tablespoons olive oil
- 1 tablespoon chives, chopped
- 1 tablespoon rosemary, chopped
- Black pepper to the taste

Directions:
1. Put the mushrooms in a roasting pan, add the oil and the rest of the ingredients, toss, bake at 400 degrees F for 25 minutes, divide into bowls and serve as a snack.

Nutrition facts per serving: calories 215, fat 12.3, fiber 6.7, carbs 15.3, protein 3.5

Black Beans and Coconut Spread

Prep time: 5 minutes I **Cooking time:** 0 minutes I **Servings:** 4

Ingredients:
- ½ cup coconut cream
- 1 tablespoon olive oil
- 2 cups black beans, cooked
- 2 tablespoons green onions, chopped

Directions:
1. In a blender, combine the beans with the cream and the other ingredients, pulse well, divide into bowls and serve.

Nutrition facts per serving: calories 311, fat 13.5, fiber 6, carbs 18.0, protein 8

Chili and Fennel Bowls

Prep time: 5 minutes I **Cooking time:** 0 minutes I **Servings:** 4

Ingredients:
- 2 spring onion, chopped
- 2 fennel bulbs, shredded
- 1 green chili pepper, chopped
- 1 tomato, chopped
- 1 teaspoon turmeric powder
- 1 teaspoon lime juice
- 2 tablespoons coriander, chopped
- Black pepper to the taste

Directions:
1. In a salad bowl, mix the fennel with the onions and the other ingredients, toss, divide into cups and serve.

Nutrition facts per serving: calories 310, fat 11.5, fiber 5.1, carbs 22.3, protein 6.5

Sprouts Bites

Prep time: 10 minutes I **Cooking time:** 25 minutes I **Servings:** 4

Ingredients:
- 1 pound Brussels sprouts, trimmed and halved
- 2 tablespoons olive oil
- 1 tablespoon cumin, ground
- 1 cup dill, chopped
- 2 garlic cloves, minced

Directions:
1. In a roasting pan, combine the Brussels sprouts with the oil and the other ingredients, toss and bake at 390 degrees F for 25 minutes.
2. Divide the sprouts into bowls and serve as a snack.

Nutrition facts per serving: calories 270, fat 10.3, fiber 5.2, carbs 11.1, protein 6

Walnuts Snack

Ingredients:
- 2 cups walnuts
- 3 tablespoons red vinegar
- A drizzle of olive oil
- A pinch of cayenne pepper
- A pinch of red pepper flakes
- Black pepper to the taste

Directions:
1. Spread the walnuts on a lined baking sheet, add the vinegar and the other ingredients, toss, and roast at 400 degrees F for 15 minutes.
2. Divide the walnuts into bowls and serve.

Nutrition facts per serving: calories 280, fat 12.2, fiber 2, carbs 15.8, protein 6

Radish Chips

Ingredients:
- 1 pound radishes, thinly sliced
- A pinch of turmeric powder
- Black pepper for taste
- 2 tablespoons olive oil

Directions:
1. Spread the radish chips on a lined baking sheet, add the oil and the other ingredients, toss and bake at 400 degrees F for 20 minutes.
2. Divide the chips into bowls and serve.

Nutrition facts per serving: calories 120, fat 8.3, fiber 1, carbs 3.8, protein 6

Leeks Bowls

Prep time: 4 minutes I **Cooking time:** 0 minutes I **Servings:** 4

Ingredients:
- 4 leeks, sliced
- 1 cup cilantro, chopped
- Juice of 1 lime
- 1 tablespoon lime zest, grated
- 1 cup cherry tomatoes, halved
- 2 tablespoons olive oil
- Salt and black pepper to the taste

Directions:
1. In a salad bowl, mix the leeks and the other ingredients, toss, divide into small cups and serve.

Nutrition facts per serving: calories 280, fat 9.1, fiber 5.2, carbs 12.6, protein 5

Creamy Leeks Dip

Prep time: 5 minutes I **Cooking time:** 0 minutes I **Servings:** 4

Ingredients:
- 1 tablespoon lemon juice
- ½ cup cream cheese
- 2 tablespoons olive oil
- Black pepper to the taste
- 4 leeks, chopped
- 1 tablespoon cilantro, chopped

Directions:
1. In a blender, combine the cream cheese with the leeks and the other ingredients, pulse well, divide into bowls and serve as a party dip.

Nutrition facts per serving: calories 300, fat 12.2, fiber 7.6, carbs 14.7, protein 5.6

Peppers Cups

Prep time: 5 minutes I **Cooking time:** 0 minutes I **Servings:** 4

Ingredients:
- ½ pound red bell pepper, cut into thin strips
- 3 green onions, chopped
- 1 tablespoon olive oil
- 2 teaspoons ginger, grated
- ½ teaspoon rosemary, dried
- 3 tablespoons balsamic vinegar

Directions:
1. In a salad bowl, mix the bell peppers with the onions and the other ingredients, toss, divide into small cups and serve.

Nutrition facts per serving: calories 160, fat 6, fiber 3, carbs 10.9, protein 5.2

Coconut Avocado Spread

Prep time: 4 minutes I **Cooking time:** 0 minutes I **Servings:** 4

Ingredients:
- 2 tablespoons dill, chopped
- 1 shallot, chopped
- 2 garlic cloves, minced
- 2 avocados, peeled, pitted and chopped
- 1 cup coconut cream
- 2 tablespoons olive oil
- 2 tablespoons lime juice
- Black pepper to the taste

Directions:
1. In a blender, combine the avocados with the shallots, garlic and the other ingredients, pulse well, divide into small bowls and serve as a snack.

Nutrition facts per serving: calories 300, fat 22.3, fiber 6.4, carbs 42, protein 8.9

Lemon Corn Dip

Prep time: 30 minutes I **Cooking time:** 0 minutes I **Servings:** 4

Ingredients:
- A pinch of cayenne pepper
- A pinch of black pepper
- 2 cups corn
- 1 cup coconut cream
- 2 tablespoons lemon juice
- 2 tablespoon avocado oil

Directions:
1. In a blender, combine the corn with the cream and the other ingredients, pulse well, divide into bowls and serve as a party dip.

Nutrition facts per serving: calories 215, fat 16.2, fiber 3.8, carbs 18.4, protein 4

Beans and Chia Power Bars

Prep time: 2 hours I **Cooking time:** 0 minutes I **Servings:** 12

Ingredients:
- 1 cup black beans, cooked
- 1 cup coconut flakes, unsweetened
- 1 cup butter
- ½ cup chia seeds
- ½ cup coconut cream

Directions:
1. In a blender, combine the beans with the coconut flakes and the other ingredients, pulse well, spread this into a square pan, press, keep in the fridge for 2 hours, slice into medium bars and serve.

Nutrition facts per serving: calories 141, fat 7, fiber 5, carbs 16.2, protein 5

Apple Chips Mix

Prep time: 10 minutes I **Cooking time:** 2 hours I **Servings:** 4

Ingredients:
- Cooking spray
- 2 teaspoons nutmeg, ground
- 1 cup pumpkin seeds
- 2 apples, cored and thinly sliced

Directions:
1. Arrange the pumpkin seeds and the apple chips on a lined baking sheet, sprinkle the nutmeg all over, grease them with the spray, introduce in the oven and bake at 300 degrees F for 2 hours.
2. Divide into bowls and serve as a snack.

Nutrition facts per serving: calories 80, fat 0, fiber 3, carbs 7, protein 4

Yogurt Dip

Prep time: 5 minutes I **Cooking time:** 0 minutes I **Servings:** 4

Ingredients:
- 2 cups Greek yogurt
- 1 tablespoon parsley, chopped
- ¼ cup tomatoes, chopped
- 2 tablespoons chives, chopped
- Black pepper to the taste

Directions:
1. In a bowl, mix the yogurt with the parsley and the other ingredients, whisk well, divide into small bowls and serve as a party dip.

Nutrition facts per serving: calories 78, fat 0, fiber 0.2, carbs 10.6, protein 8.2

Beet Bites

Prep time: 10 minutes I **Cooking time:** 35 minutes I **Servings:** 2

Ingredients:
- 1 teaspoon cayenne pepper
- 2 beets, peeled and cubed
- 1 teaspoon rosemary, dried
- 1 tablespoon olive oil
- 2 teaspoons lime juice

Directions:
1. In a roasting pan, combine the beet bites with the cayenne and the other ingredients, toss, introduce in the oven, roast at 355 degrees F for 35 minutes, divide into small bowls and serve as a snack.

Nutrition facts per serving: calories 170, fat 12.2, fiber 7, carbs 15.1, protein 6

Pecans Bowls

Prep time: 10 minutes I **Cooking time:** 10 minutes I **Servings:** 4

Ingredients:
- 2 cup walnuts
- 1 cup pecans, chopped
- 1 teaspoon avocado oil
- ½ teaspoon sweet paprika

Directions:·
1. Spread the grapes and pecans on a lined baking sheet, add the oil and the paprika, toss, and bake at 400 degrees F for 10 minutes.
2. Divide into bowls and serve as a snack.

Nutrition facts per serving: calories 220, fat 12.4, fiber 3, carbs 12.9, protein 5.6

Salmon Muffins

Prep time: 10 minutes I **Cooking time:** 25 minutes I **Servings:** 4

Ingredients:
- 1 cup mozzarella cheese, shredded
- 8 ounces smoked salmon, skinless, boneless, and chopped
- 1 cup almond flour
- 1 egg, whisked
- 1 teaspoon parsley, dried
- 1 garlic clove, minced
- Black pepper to the taste
- Cooking spray

Directions:
1. In a bowl, combine the salmon with the mozzarella and the other ingredients except the cooking spray and stir well.
2. Divide this mix into a muffin tray greased with the cooking spray, bake in the oven at 375 degrees F for 25 minutes and serve as a snack.

Nutrition facts per serving: calories 273, fat 17, fiber 3.5, carbs 6.9, protein 21.8

Squash Bites

Prep time: 10 minutes I **Cooking time:** 20 minutes I **Servings:** 8

Ingredients:
- A drizzle of olive oil
- 1 big butternut squash, peeled and minced
- 2 tablespoons cilantro, chopped
- 2 eggs, whisked
- ½ cup whole wheat flour
- Black pepper to the taste
- 2 shallots, chopped
- 2 garlic cloves, minced

Directions:
1. In a bowl, mix the squash with the cilantro and the other ingredients except the oil, stir well and shape medium balls out of this mix.
2. Arrange them on a lined baking sheet, grease them with the oil, bake at 400 degrees F for 10 minutes on each side, divide into bowls and serve.

Nutrition facts per serving: calories 78, fat 3, fiber 0.9, carbs 10.8, protein 2.7

Green Beans Snack Bowls

Prep time: 10 minutes I **Cooking time:** 30 minutes I **Servings:** 8

Ingredients:

- 1 pound green beans, trimmed
- 3 tablespoons parsley, chopped
- 1 tablespoon chives, chopped
- Black pepper to the taste
- 1 cup mozzarella, grated
- 1 tablespoon olive oil

Directions:

1. Spread the beans on a lined baking sheet, add the oil, parsley, chives and the black pepper and toss.
2. Sprinkle the mozzarella on top, bake at 390 degrees F for 30 minutes, divide into bowls and serve cold as a snack.

Nutrition facts per serving: calories 136, fat 2.7, fiber 6, carbs 25.9, protein 4.1

Broccoli and Shrimp Bars

Prep time: 10 minutes I **Cooking time:** 25 minutes I **Servings:** 8

Ingredients:
- 1 pound broccoli florets, chopped
- ½ pound shrimp, peeled, deveined and chopped
- ½ cup mozzarella cheese, shredded
- 2 eggs, whisked
- 1 teaspoon oregano, dried
- 1 teaspoon basil, dried
- Black pepper to the taste

Directions:
1. In a bowl, mix the broccoli with the cheese and the other ingredients, stir well, spread into a rectangle pan and press well on the bottom.
2. Introduce in the oven at 380 degrees F, bake for 25 minutes, cut into bars and serve cold.

Nutrition facts per serving: calories 46, fat 1.3, fiber 1.8, carbs 4.2, protein 5

Pineapple and Basil Salsa

Prep time: 10 minutes I **Cooking time:** 40 minutes I **Servings:** 4

Ingredients:
- 20 ounces pineapple, cubed
- 1 cup sun-dried tomatoes, cubed
- 3 tablespoons basil, chopped
- 1 tablespoon avocado oil
- 1 teaspoon lime juice
- 1 cup black olives, pitted and sliced
- Black pepper to the taste

Directions:
1. In a bowl, combine the pineapple cubes with the tomatoes and the other ingredients, toss, divide into smaller cups and serve as a snack.

Nutrition facts per serving: calories 125, fat 4.3, fiber 3.8, carbs 23.6, protein 1.5

CPSIA information can be obtained
at www.ICGtesting.com
Printed in the USA
LVHW020247210121
677073LV00010B/500

9 781801 577878